# ORPHANS OF THE REAL

## REFLECTIONS ON LOVE AND LOSS

ORPHANS OF THE REAL
By Marilyn Charles

Designer: Kelly Ludwig
Cover Illustration: Marilyn Charles



Readers are encouraged to go to www.MissionPointPress.com to contact the author or to find information on how to buy this book in bulk at a discounted rate.

Published by Mission Point Press
Traverse City, MI 49696
www.MissionPointPress.com

ISBN Hardcover: 978-1-968761-79-0
ISBN Softcover: 978-1-968761-80-6
Library of Congress Control Number:
2026910069
Printed in the United States of America

# ORPHANS OF THE REAL

## REFLECTIONS ON LOVE AND LOSS

MARILYN CHARLES

# *Other Books by Marilyn Charles*

*Patterns: Building Blocks of Experience* (The Analytic Press)

*Learning From Experience: A Guidebook for Clinicians* (The Analytic Press)

*Constructing Realities: Transformations through Myth and Metaphor* (Rodopi)

*Working with Trauma: Lessons from Bion and Lacan* (Jason Aronson)

*Psychoanalysis and Literature: The Stories We Live* (Rowman & Littlefield)

*Introduction to Contemporary Psychoanalysis: Defining Terms and Building Bridges* (Relational Perspectives Book Series)

*Echoes of Trauma: Meaning and Identity in Psychoanalysis* (APA Press)

*Fragments of Trauma and the Social Production of Suffering* with M. O'Loughlin (Rowman & Littlefield)

*The Importance of Play in Early Childhood Education: Psychoanalytic, Attachment, and Developmental Perspectives* with J. Bellinson (Routledge)

*Women and the Psychosocial Construction of Madness* with M.H. Brown (Rowman & Littlefield)

*Women & Psychosis: Multidisciplinary Perspectives* with M.H. Brown (Rowman & Littlefield)

# *Contents*

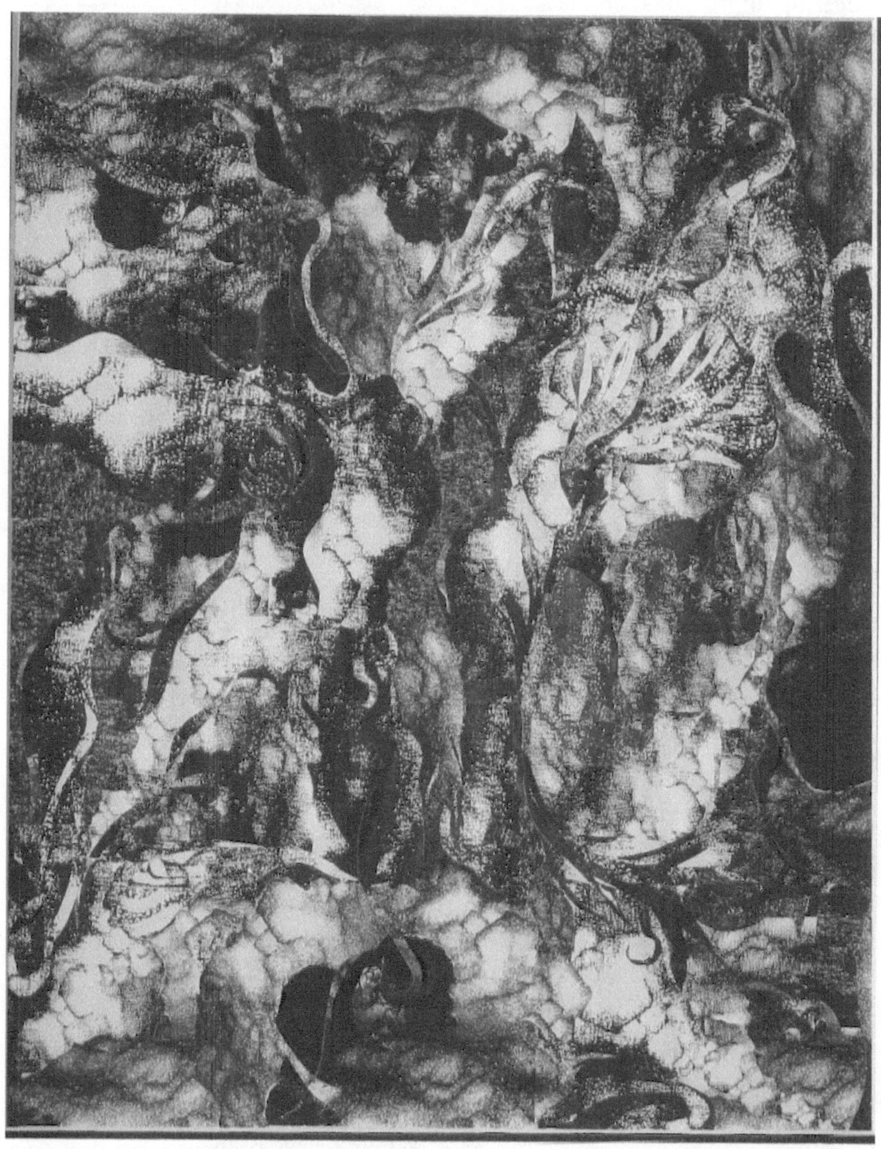

"Ascension"
Collage by Marilyn Charles

# *Foreword to Marilyn Charles'* Orphans of the Real

In her book-length poem, *Orphans of the Real*, Marilyn Charles combines fragments of self-experience into a spellbinding adventure as she strives to integrate a mosaic of loss and memory into a stream of consciousness and sustain it over time. The poems build upon one another to a crescendo, revealing the self as through a white light, a prism, shifted from one side to another, seen from many perspectives, and many facets of time. Traumatized by the death of her young son, Charles opens the floodgates of emotions while seeking meaning in a world where she has been orphaned, as a mother, searching for her dead child while seeking protection from a mother who failed her by not really seeing or understanding her. Thus, there are multiple orphans in this collection: the mother of the poet who orphaned her daughter, the poet/mother orphaned by the death of a child, and the grieving mother orphaned by life itself. The language itself has no beginning or end but, through repeated iterations, creates a path through the forest of her bewilderment, as she tries to make sense of her own existence in time.

The maternal archetype flows through waves of love and attachment. An orphan, through the breaching of the maternal dyad, is unattached, has no home, nothing to belong to. Charles, by relinquishing her attachment to her own personal mother, addressing her as a separate self, through transferences and projections, reaches a transformational epiphany, overcoming the pain of grief by keeping the dead alive—creating phantoms as parts of her psychic self-structure.

Marilyn Charles movingly chronicles the passage of heartache and uncertainty accompanying grief. Her echoing imagination binds the wanderer and the wandered into one vibrant tapestry. She challenges many assumptions readers make about poetry, that it must be tidy, or have formality in its lyricism, or a theme that can be interpreted or summed up; the assumption that poetry is so tangled up in the poet's private iconography that it is merely self-catharsis. Rather, poetry is a schoolhouse for emotions, and readers of the long poem dating back to the modernists and surrealists will recognize themselves in the cascading language of Charles' poetry. Language like this: "Secure your memories /Against receding footsteps / Haunting at your door" reminds us that we all have our dead for whom we yearn. We are all like that other orphan, Orpheus, descending down to Hades and bargaining for our Eurydice's return, turning back to watch as they disappear. Memories never really die in elegies, but live on.

Sorrow is measured not by the elimination of joy but by its temporary absence. This temporality permits us to bear the unbearable reality of loss. "Bear" is a homograph for "bare" and this is what Charles does, revealing the naked vulnerability of the self bearing loss. *Orphans of the Real* invites us on the poet's passage from sight to insight through the language of elegy, which is Charles' "native tongue." The beauty and intensity of Charles' sustained elegy leaves us feeling much as we do after listening to Mozart's *Requiem*, grief stricken, transformed, and exalted.

Judith Harris, PhD, is the author of three books of poetry from LSU Press and was nominated by LSU for the Pulitzer Prize in poetry. She has been a professor at George Washington University, American University, and the Catholic University of America. She is also the author of two critical books: *Signifying Pain: Writing and Healing the Self through Language* (SUNY Press) and *The Poetry of Loss: Romantic and Contemporary Elegies* (Routledge Press) and has written extensively about poetry and psychoanalysis. Her poems have appeared in *The Atlantic, The Nation, Slate, The New Republic, The New York Times* and the syndicated newspaper column, "American Life in Poetry," *The Hudson Review*, and *Harvard Review*.

# Preface

An uneasy entry into the world left me searching for solace—and meaning—in unlikely places. In a world where I could not find myself in my mother's eyes, people remained endlessly enigmatic, leaving me to travel as a lost soul, desperately seeking some other through whom I might find myself. Finding love and care, as we know, only goes so far, but it does give us a resting place in what can otherwise be a very lonely existence, indeed.

My first son's death when I was in my early thirties left me determined to put together a life from threads that had never come together into a coherent path. Suddenly, like a kaleidoscope finally coming into focus, the path lay clear. I began to grapple with the legacy left from my early life—my sense that my own truths could not hold in the face of another's—and determined to make my son's life matter.

In psychoanalysis I found, not answers, but rather a frame through which possibilities of meaning might be revealed. These poems were written during that time of earnest soul-seeking, when I plumbed my own depths and moved beyond what even my very caring analyst might hold. When my analysis exploded, quite magnificently, that enactment mirrored, of course, my early entry into being. But we could not hold it then, together, and I was left to wander my path alone.

The journey into self-analysis was equipped by the tools I had gathered, leading me to grapple, once again, with the need to discover and stand with and speak from my own truths, particularly when they conflicted with those of others. In these efforts, we see the journey towards reclaiming one's own soul through the development of our reflective capacities. This, I think, is the proper province of the psychoanalytic passage.

In these pages, I offer you the reflections culled from my immersion into my own primary process, what I call the aesthetic underbelly of experience, hoping they might speak to you at that level and invite something of value for you as well.

At best, poetry, like all art, speaks from the universal through the individual. In sharing our voices and our visions, as best we might, we celebrate the possibilities of becoming more than we had envisioned, as we follow the path of the soul.

# *Chasm*

Caught in a dance
  silent and unspoken
words of connection;
urgent passion   meeting
inattention; ebbing
  sorrowful and ashamed
  as you turn   to grasp
my waiting hand
alone
and unheeded.

Ensnared in a web
meeting only vestiges
of old selves
cast in my path
like snake skins
discarded
long before—
half-remembered—
yet alien
somehow.

They fit, painfully
as blithely, blind to me,
you weave life strands of me
Brittle fragment
Evanescent image.

I would love to jump the chasm
and stand with you
at the edge of the abyss.

Tell me stories of now, mother.
Stories edged in pain
shrouded in fear
and laced in unseen tears
of standing naked in our grief
at reaching out
for the mirrored gaze
and touching only empty shards
as wisps of ghosts crumble
into echoes of the past.

Caught in the asynchrony
—out of key—
Hopes swell; and break
on familiar cliffs; receding,
abashed and pummeled
by waves of connection
ambient passion; silent
and unspoken.

# *Lingering Impressions*

I think I write
because the written word seems solid—
easier to hold on to.
The spoken word dissipates
  so quickly

Hard to know
What was said
What was meant
  only lingering impressions.

I keep your messages sometimes,
To see what you really said
Reassure myself
  that it was as it seemed

But it often isn't.
Some decay in the tape, perhaps,
erased the tone I detected.
Or was it only wistfulness
  that colored it that way.

She sounded upset, I say—
More a question
than a statement—
  I can't hear it any longer—

Had I been mistaken?
But no, he can hear the traces—
Imperceptible to me now.
  So hard to hold on to anything.

There was a word—
I think it was "amazing"
The extraordinary tone caught me,
  but eroded with each replay

till I could no longer be sure
and finally erased it with all the rest
Last night. After everything died
  in that stillness.

Never quite dead, it seems
Always embers in the ashes
They flare
  unexpectedly

Almost imperceptibly, at times,
Fanned by stray breezes of neglect
Or enflamed
  by a passing squall

It always takes one back a bit
That what had seemed to be
No longer is.
  One was so terribly sure, after all.

I can no longer believe
the word was there
or meant what it felt
  I know it gave me hope—and shame—

Covered by those other words—
Testaments to the narcissism
that gives rise to such nausea
  in us both.

Abashed—head down—face flames.
You were right—
of course.
  Error is easier to forgive.

And so these words
become a tribute to yours
Emblazoned as they are
across my night sky.

# *In Your Dream*

I wandered into your dream
but the sets had faded
the paper torn
in shreds, in places,
exposing bare glimpses
of other lives, papering
the walls, under and over
leaving, finally,
no trace.

The interior is dark
and overhung;
the path obscured
by ancient vines—rooting
into underbrush
  timeless traps
for unsuspecting ankles

Vision has no power
against this pervasive odor
rising from the rotting passing
of fecund leavings

No light beckons
only the filtering
of darkness in the distance
  particles of memory
almost called into being—
  radiance warming flesh

So real then,
as though it might
permeate my being
and take root there
  filling the fibers
and emanating forth
  in turn

I drink from the ebbing river
and recall those blinding flashes
with memory dimmed
by darkness.

# *Acceptance*

I try to meet

the parts that trouble me.
To accept what is—
To meet the given.

Holding a candle
to the walls
of that dark cave—
to illuminate—define
the space that is—
to take its measure—
and learn to move
within the dance.

But what is lost
is what *might* be
beyond the edges given.

Acceptance,
a two-edged sword—
allows and precludes,
at times,
but also offers passage
beyond our bounds
into what might be—
freely chosen.

How to reconcile
that in you with
that in me
without doing violence
to either
in the face of
that shattering leap
toward what can only be known
by faith.

Knowing, even so,
that the child of faith
is strong and sinewy
while the life breathes through her
yet scatters, as dust,
as it ebbs.

# *Bound as I Am*

Bound as I am
by this image of myself
Bred in a world
that contrived to create me
in some haphazard
but determined fashion—
I have looked for you
in all my favorite hiding places
I have called to you
my passwords
and passed to you
my keys.

I have asked of you
the impossible—
That the impossible
might be
  finally
  inexorably
brought to fruition
in all its ultimate
majesty

With trumpet call—
in measured step;
The processional arrives
at your throne
Your gown arranged
in claret folds
of velvet draping
to the floor

As dreamed once
  long ago
in that great hall
Ladies in waiting,
  attending.

My attention taken,
I recede, and watch
from that cold distance
as the space fills
and is no longer.

Quixotic universe
creating holes
  that can't contain,
vacuums that can't be filled.

Matter with no place
No matter
The void has no face
from which might spill
a tear.
No tears for that
which was—
  *Is not* becomes the only truth
  *Is not* becomes you.

Comes your glass
as ladies waiting
coil round you
Viper's tresses,
hidden now
The visage
that you might have seen
  lost
under layers of deceit
  veils of illusion
never penetrated.

I have searched for you
  in my most cherished sanctuaries
I have reached for you
  in your absence
I have called your name
  silently
knowing you would not hear.

Yet needing to try.
Just in case.
One never knows
when the magic
might be about.

One hopes
One waits
One sails boats
down the river
towards some distant sea

Sodden missives
disintegrating
just beyond sight
Sailing valiantly past
the slumbering god
who awakens refreshed
  at ready
  out of time
  out of synch
like music played
too slowly,
grinding down,
to its absence.

# *Mother Superior*

Mother Superior
drapes her smile
in vestments black
as the guests arrive
at the feast—
chamber of the bride
  festooned in garlands
  of red and white.

Behind veiled eyes
  sightless
in their unwillingness
to yield
to a new era
come upon her
  so suddenly
  without warning

Leaning over the balcony
  desperately
  hungrily
pulling in air—
breaths tainted
by the fragrance
of roses climbing
towards her.

Full lush petals—
the promise of life
  held forth
  yet lurking
beyond the sting
of thorns,
should one dare
to grasp for more.

Grown over now,
to thicket formed.
Cast out, as she
eschews the light
*taken*, though given
freely, until outshone,
  glowing sun
  to her pale moon.

Silence now,
save faint shadows
of refrain, wafting
through the years;
sweet agony of despair
for all that withers
on the vine

Untasted fruit
of some distant summer,
  receding from view
  in the heat of a new season.

Banished
by her own refusal
to embrace
this strange new life.
Destiny completes itself
announcing this old cycle—
beginning anew.

Mother Superior
  vestments black
draping folds
  mirroring
darker pools
  of eyes
once sparkled
  by some new vision

Drowning now
in her own
necessity.

Marilyn Charles

# *Caught*

Too caught by what is not
to accept what is
Wounded still
by sins of omission
  commission

I have walked with you
at the edges of eternity
looking down the chasms
of repeating patterns
Ritual sacrifice
  of that poorly loved daughter

We have drunk from cool waters
terrifying in their depth
Once clear; polluted now
by poisoned fragments
of arrows flung
in blind defense
  from that small enemy

I see you glisten
through the dense heat
of summer's day
oil on pavement
  shimmering rainbows
dissipating
  with decreasing distance

Feeling now
the urgency of your heart
moving toward me
calling for acceptance
amidst the rubble
of half-forgotten dreams
  merging into uncertainty

gathering round me
once again.
Remembered warmth
enfolds me, until
the knife twist
  pierces the dream.

# *Self Portrait*

No one seemed to see the pain
so she tried to portray it
in ways they might understand
  gathering swirling specks of colored air,
  playing internal agonies and ecstasies
across the fields of her imaginings;
Weaving images from currents of despair
into piercing harmonies,
chords played on threads—stretched
from the gutted strings of sorrow

She has played them for so long
  their ancestry has dimmed
into some remote and veiled past
  shrouded now
as though created from
some twisted self-indulgence,
  roots emerging from evil desires
lurking neath the sheer surface of her agony

And so she fouls her own memory
Faith becomes one more treachery
of a spirit damned by lack of kindness
  taken into itself, as its own,
  fed by that unknown spring
whose need must deny her own
  moving her further into darkness
Subterranean passages carrying her destiny
  sealed by the blindness exacted for survival

# *Time's Line*

Part of me lies on that hillside with you
Body become spirit
emptying into that cold earth
Skies looming large with black clouds
  portending violence
  imminent in that still air.

A time when anything could happen
perched as it was
between those two worlds
  of before   and after
One moment came   and went unnoticed
  moving forever   into after
Days spent trying to move back   into before
trying to find that moment   before you left
trying to understand   how life can leave

Rocking, keening, to the rhythm of all
that can never be absorbed
  into a woman's womb
Flesh of her flesh no more;
blood of her blood
  trickled long since
into tiny crevasses of the earth's crust;
can no more be called back
than life could be called forth
from that moment   when time stopped
and stood still   and refused to move
backward   to before

Moments called to memory
as though they could be reclaimed
moving ever backward
like a blind diver through dark waters
searching for the path
that became tangled and lost
but must remain
—if only we could find it
—if it weren't so hard to see.

Moving backward, acts undone,
as though that would be the very one—
the magic incantation to release the chain
and send it forward to its rightful end—
reverse this moment that cannot be

I long to breathe my life back
  into that waiting body
and puzzle over the line   between
existence   and eternity
which you passed   without telling me
  knowing I would hold you here

Holding you
in my nonacceptance
  of what cannot be
as though I could redo the tale
to some better ending
and you would be beside me
gazing up, smiling at my silliness

as you often did
when I was lost in my grown up world
leaving so little room
for the present moment
  which passed unnoticed
  while I sat unaware
of the line being crossed
on that bleak hill

or how valiantly I would try to move it
back   to before
to find that moment
  when all was not lost
  before all was lost
trickling into the crevasses
of cold earth   distant now,
yet ever present

My heart skips backward
across that line
like a child's magic.

Empty gesture of futility
without the faith
  that might
bring the magic to life
crossing backward   over time
  to that line
  sealed now,
deep within the shifting sand
that shrouds the hill.

Marilyn Charles

# *Digging*

Digging in the earth in that time between night and morning
alone, yet not alone, in the stillness of the stars and moon
carrying within me the seeds of your beginnings;
too frightened to sleep, wondering, what manner
of mother I might be
to this boy child within.

Looking back, through the passing of time
at that lonely figure, digging against destiny;
digging against the day too soon
when she would be digging again
burying what was left of the child conceived that night.
It seems I knew, in some part of me,
I could not hold on to this child, both longed for and feared
  having been humbled already
  in the face of motherhood.

I had invoked one more accusing gaze
and yet could do no other,
propelled by the force of my longing
for the child I could never hold
but escaped laughing through my grasp—
Though you let me hold you for some brief time,
you slipped through my fingers like grains of sand;
Your reality disappearing like faery dust
  with the passing time.

I dig in my garden, hunched with the weight
of all women   who bury their sons
in their sweat   and their tears
Consoled by their presence;   alone
  in the fortress of my grief.

Leaves have fallen from the trees.
I sow seeds toward that distant spring
  which has been rumored
  though I no longer believe in it;
and yet move toward it   as inevitably
as I dug in that garden long ago
planting nothing—

For all that mattered
had been planted   toward the time
when neither my sun   nor my rain
could give it life again.

# *Ancestry*

Mother of my spirit
Bequeather of legends
that stir in me
memories of distant pasts
I dimly see in dreams

Remote fathers with visage turned,
barely perceptible in the harsh light
by eyes more accustomed to the dim interiors
of downturned heads, ministering and mourning
their dying mothers and needy children

Children grinding spices on some shrouded verandah
The smells rising toward a future imaged across the horizon
Scrubbing away the sins of their ancestors—
the mark of difference and nonbelonging
that kept them wandering in search of home

Shelter having been the womb of sorrows
woven in tapestries of despair
hardened at its outer core toward survival,
obliged and determined to carry forward
toward some vague promise of redemption

I have known you in the deepest recesses of my being.
I have renounced you, turned aside, and cast you out,
yet you live within me; spinning stories of long ago
and far away—beginnings of these images that haunt
my waking sleep and color all my dreams

Written in the cells constructing me,
you speak to me of hope smashed and love tested
to intolerable limits
I have stood in your showers of death and lain in your dark ovens
my bones mingled with remains of others' dreams
devoured in the flames of another blind dragon

I have looked through your eyes and wondered
at your fear of being seen in hate's cruel light
annihilated by alien eyes distorted by fear
The fear my heritage too—of safety through invisibility
Preservation through self-annihilation

Mother of my being
I lie each night in your embrace
as you whisper within
stirring winds of ashes scattered long ago
into images coiled   within the wombs of future generations.

# *Unknown Beaches*

Striding blindly over unknown beaches
crushing shells beneath my feet
demolishing ancestral homes
once inhabited, now suspended
into some eternal question

In our arrogance, we destroy
vast civilizations
under feet unfeeling in their purpose
numb to unheard cries
of erstwhile travelers unheeded

So attuned to inner keening
deadened to outer reverberations
of pain affirmed and echoed
in eyes saddened by blindness
leaving no hope of shelter there

In rooms cold and bare
sheerest curtains swelling
to whispered breeze of memories
calling sweetly for admittance
to that realm of hidden dreams

Wandering through empty rectangles
Evanescent images of spaces
once inhabited by unknown ancestors
I wander through open doorways
in search of something once forgotten

Memories of footfalls—
the trail of some diaphanous gown
almost glimpsed—dimly—
rustling  far from view—
beyond the next passage

So many nights spent wandering
amidst tarnished relics
heaped in disarray
amassed in some ancestral shrine
to the living

I lead you through this mausoleum
seeking out treasures
worth reclaiming from the dust
of ages passed—and passing now
beneath my troubled gaze

No assurance here
only the certainty of meaning
in an unknown form
carried intact in this vessel
long since sealed

Yet waiting still
in hope of redemption
for an unknown sin
  long forgotten
  forever atoned

In these empty spaces
pregnant with the promise
of life unlived
waiting for conception
to carry me from within

My prison of half-imaged spaces
relics of antiquity
sought through dreams
long forgotten
in distant twilit sleep

# *The Siege*

The long siege ended
as supplies ran low
hunger a dim memory,
rumbling—distant thunder

No one claimed victory
flanked as they were
by groans of the dying
strewn randomly o'er the hill

But sat as if captured
by the war engaged by passion,
struggling to recall—what matter
of import gathered them there

At once stunned and chastened
at the carnage rendered
eyes withdrawn in shame—and disbelief
at the victims' trusting stares

Trying to recall the enemy
beneath the mirrored visage
so like our own
cut against a different cloth

I have searched for you
through the night of distant hillsides
in the darkness of my fear
with bayonet drawn

I have hunted you
'cross fields steaming with still departing life
To steal that breath from you
my solitary aim

And now sit foolishly
two captains become boys again
chagrined at being caught
absorbed in childish games

We sit sentinels
to that dark purpose
that gathers sons and brothers unto itself
to no end save vanity.

Marilyn Charles

# *Twilit Creatures*

You move into that zone of twilit creatures
dimly perceived across the vastness of space and time
Safe upon your weighty throne
in the land of sacramental dreams

Characters converging, clothed in new array
familiar beneath the mantle of particulars
Gathering for the storm that plays itself out
in new detail on each successive day

They mass, waiting, interconnected yet alone—
players on a chessboard, awaiting orders.
You move into that space of sweeping visions
as I assemble for you my armament of images

And feel you recede into that world beyond time
alone with the specters and remoteness of your being.
We do battle to secure this tower of truth
where all may be known in tandem solitude

Illusion of intimacy thrown on time's wheel
spinning wildly out of control
Fighting to reach this fortress of repose
within the imminent darkening storm

Where we might take in the terrain of despair
from the safety of these soothing walls.
I move inexorably towards the crack in the tower
from which I am forever expelled

Until I sit calmly at your feet, fervor spent
in disbelief at such nearness—out of reach
Grief moves into emptiness, light enough now
to traverse these tempered distant spaces

# *Changing Houses*

You say you change houses like realities;
a new one each year

I don't understand.

Mine grows round me laboriously
like the shell of some crustacean
over tiny eternities

Coiling me in ever widening spirals,
enticements of beauty
in protective barriers

Thinly veiled by finely fashioned membrane
encrusted with jewels
gathered from the deep

Treasures wrested from nightly explorations
in the mystery of spaces
revealed in dreams

I go wandering through silent empty halls
with lightly curtained windows
lit by distant whispering breeze

Endless conceptions of corridors so familiar
their presence welcomes me
in warm embrace

Promising everything, yet out of reach
elusive whispers on an air
of something long forgotten

Glancing by, toward some remote oblivion
leaving in its wake only half-remembered promises
emerging ancestral home, unrequited

# *Ceasefire*

I saw you yesterday
for the first time
since the war ended
and we found ourselves
in non-neutral corners
separated by a wall
we could not scale
from either side.

I had known I would see you
and hoped to survive
without meeting face to face
  walls of pain
tightening bands across my chest.

I thought I was not thinking about it
but recognized my rising fear
in my frenetic pace
  mounting as the time neared
for seeing and not meeting.

I thought perhaps you might not come
having glimpsed your face
hardened  by time and distance
  days before, when you were busy
not-seeing me.

But I saw you yesterday
for the first time since the war ended
and the armies retreated
  to pick through the ashes
defeated and puzzled

by pieces that would never fit
but could only lie in fragments
till ploughed deeply
  into graves marked only
by remembrance.

I could see your shape across the room
turned away intently
towards some other
  as I stole through the crowd
to find a place of refuge.

I tried not to care but my attention slipped
to you, standing in your space, and I in mine.
I almost escaped, till I neared the door
  and saw you standing there,
lying in wait.

It was nothing, just hello,
a mere acknowledgement
of one being to another;
  pretence of contact, where there is none
without pain.

You had no right.
You should have known.
but then, you hadn't known me
for a very long time.

Perhaps that was the battlefield
on which the war was fought
in the first place
over who might know what
  about whom
  and when.

You should have known.
But then, perhaps you did,
and it didn't matter any more
in the same way

Rules of war
no longer in effect
giving way
to conditions of non-engagement.

I thought I might see you yesterday
and hoped I would survive
apparently unscathed.
But we were playing by different rules.

I should have known.
But then, I hadn't known you
for a very long time.

# *Waiting to Be Spoken*

My feelings well
waiting to be spoken
  shared
embraced and imbibed
in their fullness
enlivening
the space
between.

I wonder at the press
to bring you in,
  enfold you
  be enfolded by you
in this vast ocean
where edges blur
and become permeable
as sensation becomes
palpable emanations
whose source is lost
in the power of feeling
passing now between us;
highly charged current
barely contained.

*We* are barely contained
rocked to our very foundations
  any power an illusion
in the face of this force, of us
  yet more than us
a gift of sorts
like life itself
to be channeled
for good or ill.

To lose it, unthinkable—
evokes my fiercest self,
  protecting you
  soothing me
bringing us back
to equilibrium
as though we had created
some strange embryo of the senses
through which to abide
  for a time
and so sustain our selves.

That other self I know so deeply
engages my curiosity
for I hardly know you at all
only what you show me
from behind the mask, wrought
of whatever parts you—
  whatever parts me—
keep it fixed in place.

I write to be with you
to keep alive this feeling
that fills an empty part of me—
  almost unnoticed
until you entered there.

Taken by surprise
at the intensity of feeling
as you began to permeate
my waking thoughts and dreams
pulling my attention—my senses—
until I caught myself in waiting
and stared at my anticipation
donned like the crisp frock
of a schoolgirl for the new teacher.

What *is* this,
evoked in me
I have seen it in others
and wonder what that means
unwilling to be
one more acolyte, basking
in your benevolent gaze.

You speak to me in certainties
unraveling into mysteries
in your absence
as fear filters through the cracks
of what might have been known.

I search for some certainty
you have no way to give me
nor I the right to ask
  ironic betrayal of all externals
in this mystic, healing union
that defies all will or intention
but merely is—
to be cherished or abandoned.

Desperate to make it real,
I run to you, to find you—
like the child's delight
as the mother's face reappears
from the vast terror of emptiness
in which she might bury her head
for just a moment
for the sheer delight
of meeting once again.

Your face has so many stories
shadows of light and dark
flickering across the surface
they call to me to know them
  to know you
that you might be known
and your pain lessened, shared.

I would take your hand and hold it
that you might never be alone again
but always have that warmth
of a stroke across your cheek
  or palm upon your chest
warming the emptiness
  and filling it
until you can look
into eyes that hold
and cherish you
and need nothing from you
save you be
wherever you happen to be.

I think you have lived your whole life
learning how to be
  for others
  with others
meeting some emptiness
in your own heart
by meeting theirs,
willing it to be filled
and healed
by the power of your care.

So I, in my arrogance, too,
believe I see you—
with eyes into the soul
opened by this channel
created through being with
one another
  despite the pain
toward whatever
might be.

Marilyn Charles

# *The Promise of Love*

It was really just a poem

about the promise of love
  that sweet seduction
that is everything and nothing
that never moves
beyond the being-for
into being with.

Where knowing is of the other
  for the self
where all is given
in the service of that great
mirror pool on the horizon
ever reflecting back
our most serene image
  self-infatuation most sublime.

It was supposed to be about love
that lures and beckons,
a siren's call,
  remote and omnipresent
in its stunning isolation

All pretence of defenses
  knocked out
in the face of the perfect love
that turns the key
  unlocks the shell
leaving the inner core open
to complete annihilation

In the service of what transformation
do I lie here in fragments
searching now listlessly
  now in earnest
for some key toward survival
in the face of not-being enough
to hold the siren in my gaze
but watch it recede
pulling my sorrow
beyond endurance

into what remains
in the wake of the tempest
which had been
  for some brief and eternal moment
the promise of love.

Marilyn Charles

# *Storm's Wake Passing*

I seem to have set my self
towards my own destruction
At some point the rest
will just wither and die.
Images seeking salvation
become obstacles in the path
and fall away—smile not yet faded
perplexed by the storm's wake passing.

I can't even tell
who has failed whom
only that they all failed
like misbegotten embryos
  sloughed off
in monthly cleansings
  of inner refuse
no life to offer nor contain
though love's illusion tasted sweet—for a time.

I have traveled some distance
to arrive nowhere
no where left to travel
having come to that crossing
where only I lie in my path.
Once again, I step across myself
and go on searching
for that which might be found
on some other journey.

It was never you I left behind
only your illusion of mine.
I have closed so many doors
there are none left to open
only ghosts to remind me
of what lay behind
lost in vain purging
of the inner mind.

I can see where it began to go awry
when the path home was blocked—
blockaded and distant—
  but the only path known.

At what point does renunciation
open the door once closed
by eyes willfully blind
to a child's pleas.

The door that does not open
becomes the path
  the cross carried
toward some ultimate salvation.
Not in this life time.

To set it down
and walk with empty hands
  weightless now
toward some unknown destination?
Not in this life time.

I sit at the edge of the precipice,
unsure whether it's bottom or top
or some small ledge along the way
toward falling farther
  in?
or out?

No bearings left
by which to understand
  nor cast any blame
but my own,
which turns and stands
to mock me
The rest gaze past
with whatever favor
  or distaste
is left upon their palate.

Ages pass—
only ghosts remain
  of whatever was
  or might have been—
gone into hiding
underneath—
the chosen pain
  preferable
in its blindness
to that which may not be seen
without shattering.

# *Chaos*

The chaos is gathering
  just around the edges
barely perceptible
though at times I catch it
  extending itself
if I am very still
  and pretend not to notice.

Building over moments—into years,
becoming the backdrop
of scenes cast—and re-cast
into the sea;
across the water;
set adrift
to linger there
wandering aimlessly,
in search of any scant breeze
to breathe them homeward
toward some uncertain shore.

The chaos becomes the unseen force
behind my internal velocity,
the unheard voice
whispering plots
and secret configurations
to the unseen hand
guiding footsteps
for my own blind eyes
  unfocused now
by hours spent staring
through the darkness
toward the light
staring
toward the darkness
of the light.

~ ~ ~ ~ ~

But I was talking about the chaos
before I lost my way in the darkness
before the internal chaos came—
Imperfect symmetry
mirroring the without.

It comes creeping
  unannounced
save by the whirring of its wings
  too stiff to hear
save in retrospect
  after all is lost.

It was never *that* we feared.
The true demon
was beyond imaginings
  that imperfect collaboration
of a lifetime
  intertwined upon itself;
Self-devouring, uncanny
  dance of death.

Odd ritual, this
ode to a dream
  or nightmare
riotous, frolicking
  out of control

When the pattern is played—
the leaves read,
  divined,
as they turn to ashes
  and scatter in the wind

In that moment
  glistened
a dream of life
and quickly faded
  into uncertainty.

~ ~ ~ ~ ~

But what I am trying to describe
is the chaos
that hovers 'round the edges
always threatening   to emerge,
converge   engulf   encompass me.
Remnants of a thousand years of leaving,
massing, waiting for their day,
  until what is left overwhelms

and the pressure builds
and the inside implodes
leaving only chaos and maelstrom.

These, then, are the forces of darkness, gathering
cast off demons of the night
dis-owned, denied, and bastardized
by willful blindness.

I cast out my demons, from my gut, retching,
watching, as they lie, putrefying, in wait
growing more substantial, as I divest myself
of my own substance, toward some blind eye
that soothes only for a moment
before recoiling in horror.

~ ~ ~ ~ ~

It all begins so simply
and then swirls
in the tempest of my imaginings
cursed into darkness
by all I cannot abide.
Frenzied and feverish,
babblings subside
into bastions of sorrow
embraced
then denied.

~ ~ ~ ~ ~

Somehow, it eludes me.
It veers off again
and again.

The chaos of all unattended imaginings
The dis-owned rage haunting me,
taunting me, pacing relentlessly,
seeking its way back in.

Three tries.
All failures.
To say something so simple
yet beyond words
of the terror of being revealed
and abandoned

over
and over
and over
again.

Of the rage
at speaking
  words unheard
into the emptiness
with no echo
  only the ricochet
of bullets glancing
off canyon walls.

There is no peace,
There is no order
the only rhythm
  the awful birthing
of the stillborn beast
  sucking life
from its mother's death.

No room left
  only darkness
and the fullness
of the dead child
  petrifying—inside—
in cold defiance
  of her racking rhymes.

Marilyn Charles

# *Out of Darkness*

From this hallowed ground,
Images speak   through feelings
that well and fester
searching their way   out of the darkness

I bring my images forth
or allow them their own birth
holding my breath   lest they be contaminated
by some residue of my intention

Uncertain image
caught by the barbs   of my own insides
impaled against me, tearing,
struggling to break free

Impaled image   intoned
  uncertain fragment
dirge once spoken
  against a dying light

Skin thickly floating
over lungs   filled to choking
air thick with the last embers
of droned incantations

All intent focused
last act of will
singing songs of redemption
and prayers for the dead

To suck the last breath
and expel it sighing
re-membered particles
of a lost universe

I gather myself   unto myself
waiting here   upon this altar
rocking and keening
to behold my passing.

# *Noah's Dove*

I don't know why I speak
nor to whom
only that my words cast out
like Noah's doves
seeking signs of life
in a drowning world.

I lie in the cradle of my ship
knowing only the relentless rocking
of currents hammering against the sides
as the world grows lush around me
unknown and unseen

My words carry   through moist air
and settle into new-formed land
impregnated with fragments of meaning
gleaned from fevered dreams
leaving no tomorrow
in which the dreamer wakes

Only distant futures now
with flowers plucked
and fruit eaten
full bellies left behind
in child's play,
seeds strewn across the land.

Marilyn Charles

# *Not Empty Enough*

Not empty enough
  almost
but not quite
Hard to find the balance
between emptiness and fullness
  life and death
hope and despair.

There is that point
where emptiness becomes fullness
poised as it is
  on the brink
before time resumes
its urgent rhyme.

Balanced on the edge
of empty spaces
  becoming
one
with the vastness
merging into charged particles
of light
and dark

Soaring endlessly
until time intrudes
the shadow of finity
and the image obtrudes
swallowed by its own spectre
choking on its own refuse
engorged by undigested mass

I fill the void
to persist   in time and space
losing   in its wake
the blissful union
of space within
meeting space without
merging
into infinity

Would to fill it<br>
  just enough<br>
to sustain itself<br>
  a note faltering in thin air<br>
gutted   by lack of oxygen<br>
  within?<br>
  without?<br>
It is so unclear<br>
as the particles begin to vibrate<br>
and intermingle<br>
  attenuating tendrils<br>
of desire

Longing becomes<br>
  one more danger<br>
  become vacuum<br>
waiting to be filled<br>
as the dance shifts

That which emptied<br>
becomes that which fills<br>
shifting currents<br>
  unsteady now<br>
in waves of nausea<br>
rising once again,

There is this death<br>
in life drunk too deeply,<br>
the sweetest draught<br>
saturates and smothers<br>
leaving no space left<br>
through which to breathe.

Marilyn Charles

# *Dark Promise*

Temptation's lure
  calls softly.
In her innocence
she passes through
the last outpost
circling the fortress,
climbing
spiral stairs,
dizzy with desire,
caught in the dance
  with no way back
only the steadiness
of the climb become life
  the quest become certainty
as though there were—some end
to follow.

Who stands inside
that oft imagined
door?
What joy—what evil
lurks within?
No certitude here,
only the relentless climb
toward some vision
real or imagined
as the roads entwine
like thick braids beckoning—
of hope
and fear—
desire
and despair.

Their colors mix
and sparkle
in the sun.
I am hypnotized
and lose my way
once again.
Only to find myself
once more
upon a path
so familiar
yet unknown.

I seek solace
in the air of some dim future
deeply drawn
to my breast.

It fills,
  sustains
and carries me
  to the edge of darkness
  to the edge of light
no difference here
in these upper recesses
of a castle so remote—
  barely imagined—
long forgotten

As I rock myself to sleep
on the stones
of some unknown memory
  not quite captured
in the ebbing grace
of a vaguely scented breeze
wafting outward
as it disappears.

# *Learning to Live Without You*

Learning to live without you
  practicing
in the absence of your presence, lest
in some unguarded moment
all trace should disappear
of that strange essence
marking this side of remembrance

I stand beside this yearning
toward whatever time remains
  to contain time
  as if to freeze it
in some uncertain likeness
wavering in the balance

For what
—with what—
shall I fill these last moments
  grains of sand
sifting through my fingers
leaving only empty shells
  of memories

Wisps of fragments
linger in the air
  caught
like the air of dreams
redolent yet ineffable

I can hold your likeness
but never impart it
How to trace your image
upon the eyes of unborn children
that they too might savor
its richness—so uncanny
these undreamed residues
of a life

I wonder at the portrait captured
as color met canvas
undefined, until they met headlong
Displaced, muted,
and transformed
in that meeting   until
no certainty was left
of any intent or purpose

Only empty, pointless wonderings:
Were they questions left unanswered?
or answers left unquestioned.

Marilyn Charles

# The Golem

I was thinking about the golem:
that created absence—
grotesque semblance—
creature of the void.

In the absence of the mother
the child is empty
and only appears to be alive
to those unlearned in these matters.

Tottering off to find herself,
she loses herself in every moment;
fragments of meaning strewn in her path
like droppings in the snow.

Searching for some vital spark
to carry her into being
while, in the moment,
the frame freezes.

Caught in obscure chaos,
leaving only empty platitudes
  and meaningless gestures
emanating, from vacant faces.

# *Cruel November*

In the darkening of the night
swallows sleep
in the cloak of obscurity
of dusk descended.
In the lengthening shadows
figures lurk
waiting to be startled
into some greater uncertainty.

I have searched in those moments
  as dusk settles 'round me
for some sign or symbol
to guide me unerringly
toward some greater vision
of ages past.

The cloak of November
descends chill fingers,
whispering moisture, plays
across my cheek
solitary tears escape, unshed,
almost unnoticed.

I walk the barren landscape
ripe with odors   of decaying leaves
  and unfallen snow.
Wrapped in the memories
of too many winters
to hold any.

Memory becomes a blanket
  of time untasted;
a dream escaping;
  enticing but inscrutable.

The scene sketches before me
in subtle nuances
of greys and black
smoky now in the pungency
of half-stirred memories
consumed by fire.

So easy to become lost
in a moment   between time
before hope was lost
  or refound.

My eyes close
in uneasy expectation
as snowflakes scatter,
  cross the skies
grazing softly
  my upturned brow.

# *Ice Crackles*

Ice crackles

I am all hard edges

I breathe
nascent particles
of toxic gases

I am caught
frozen
in this
harsh headlight,
carried
by guardsmen
who patrol
the border

Words are
sharp razors
on my
open target
hurling
harsh epistles
of one
night's
darkness
landing
deep frozen

And the ice
buries
locks of hair
under
light snowflakes
coiling
in sharp
surrender
to the cold
of mourning.

Marilyn Charles

# *Behind Closed Eyes*

I called you back
from where you had receded
behind closed eyes
so long ago—
the barbed wire
of stony cold silence
entrenched firmly
beneath a self-enclosing smile.

Taken by surprise—
the wrath
of closely guarded secrets
run amok—
your words pierce
my amazement
at who I had become
in your willingness
to annihilate me
even in my presence.

So deep were the wounds
I had long since
ceased to exist
as any but anathema
  for you
and stood pummeled—
gathering my senses
into my self

Then slowly,
in measured cadence
  intertwined
your voice
with mine
  bringing
my own strain
into the tune you wrought
with sharp chords of dissonance
heard through one ear.
What had seemed like melody—
reciprocal interweavings
of unique phrasings—
became void
in your accusation

of mine
as shrill counterpoint
to your own silence
as though that did not have
its own clear voice.

Two truths  became
an interweaving
of story
channeled
through blind eyes
and deadened ears
into resonance
and warm embrace
leaving wounds
to open slowly over time.

Budding tendrils
of embrace emptied
like one hand clapping
desperately trying  to capture
what had not been held
tightly enough
to keep it safe
from interpenetrations
of suspicion
and unrequited longing.

No true meeting—
the jagged edges
still too fresh—
affirmation of pain inflicted
by the absence of words
that had festered
and exploded into me
at my initiation.

# *The Sandbox*

Crouching warily, poised for battle, he waits:
face furrowed   level   with figures wedged in sand
Eyes narrowed   intent   captured by tiny titans'
bloody progress   through mythic land

Fashioning figures into convenient caricatures
to ease the torment of shades of grey.
Front lines fall   to the guttural firing
of voice become artillery:  the child at play

Apocalyptic emissions from a tiny hand, proclaim
who will be sacrificed;  who will be saved
Lost souls savagely buried, as tanks roll relentlessly
smoothing the surface of unmarked graves

Till the last battalion stands;   bowed but ready
for whatever order caprice might convey
Blind revelation:  the patriot's zeal
wreaks indifferent salvation   another game

Voyaging out over vast terrains;  in ageless boots
of timeless tread, with no clear span
Or hidden   behind fearful forays   into enemy lines
drawn and damned by an unseen hand

Driven breathless, the call relentless, toward
a future envisioned in grains of sand
His battle raging, soothed by saving
his fragile forces from alien hands.

# *Someday: A Poem in Three Voices*

Someday
I will paint you a portrait
of my son,
shown only
in black and white
with no color
to assault the eye:
glaring crimson
seeping deeply
into frozen ground

Someday
I will not show you
how the tendrils
coiled 'round his face
in the heat of whatever terror
he embraced
in those final moments
before darkness
or light
intervened

Someday
I will intone silently
so you do not hear
words emblazed in memory

(. . . there was a mark on his neck and I thought well maybe his neck had been broken and he had died very quickly because I was concerned about nobody hearing the noise in the neighborhood and the children had come out of the house very quickly and followed him but nobody heard anything. The medical investigator told me she hated to say it but the child died very slowly. The cause of death was that he bled to death and that he died very slowly; it wasn't a quick death. Her only comment could be that the child was in shock and so frightened that he couldn't make any noise.)

{But they didn't know you had practiced the art before and had never made a sound. I remember your quietness and the special note of alarm it always sounded in me, like the time I found you lying floating limp in the water: no movement: no sound. Not even a ripple of water to trace your life ebbing outward. You just let it take you. But I couldn't. I had to bring you back. Until the time when I couldn't. That odd moment when time has stopped

and erected a barrier beyond which all things must be counted anew; re-created according to the new order;
A.D.: the time of missing you.}

~~~~~

{Someday
The sight of your face
will not be fused
with the devastation
of your body}

~~~~~

Someday
I will paint you a portrait
in black and white
with only shades of grey
to mark the moments
where color had been
then slowly
ebbed away

Someday
I will paint you a portrait
of a child become unborn
ruptured into
embryonic raptures
of a life unlived
forever now

Someday
I will unpaint your sorrow
and ease the lines of care—
a picture of a universe
not lost
in despair.

# *Merlin*

Coming down from the mountain
  I feared
would transform
Merlin's wand
into a common scepter
with no power
to move.

Was that what Moses felt,
standing by the burning bush,
the flames drawing him
toward uncertain annihilation?

Some passion
  left unchecked
contains the seeds
of self-destruction
wreaked widely
  if not tempered
with regard
for those still
lying in its path

Remaining on the mountain
becomes Icarus
  falling;
wings burned
beyond hope of ever flying
  once again;
as the father watches
in helpless horror
  like Abraham
on his own peak
deafened by the thunder
  blinded by the light
his son not dead
  but sacrificed

Hard to tell saint from sinner
the only certainty
a singed feather
floating sadly
  aimlessly
where passion
had reigned

I have stood upon the mountain
urged toward flight
  felt to be reunion
toward some erstwhile mystery
  awaiting within

Certain that this wind's breath
would hold me
  in safe transport
  on this current
Dreaming my songs
into its caress
against the waking
in the chill expulsion
from the sun's embrace

All warmth receding
into the coldness
  of the fall
seen so starkly
from that high vantage
  So inevitable
  the Fall

And yet, I would climb this mountain
trading in my staff
for scepter
to command the heavens
to vouchsafe entry
into forbidden lands
where magic has no price
where the fire is eternal
the wings not waxen
the feet not clay
To not know
the betrayal
of the son
whose father stands
transfixed upon the crest

Knowing
that the not-knowing
holds within
the seeds of some
uncertain destruction
sown inevitably
  as mountains crumble
  and become sand;
illusion lost
to such abiding nakedness
  of greed unmasked
  and passion spent

The fall
was never very far away
but waited
  whispering
at the edges of the precipice
for any who would soar
too high—and unrestrained

Some journeys best untaken?
  lest we become lost
  in the dream.

# *Fugue*

This melody   haunting me
like a fugue
I can neither quite grasp
nor catch hold of

as I stand   in the stillness,
waiting, hoping
the silence will overtake me
and catch me in its thrall

to reside there,
unshaken by the soaring
streams of passions
spent in tempest's wake.

In the stillness
between passion and despair
lies the certain resolution
the struggle of the heart
to find its self
without losing its soul.

Compassion,  an icy plunge
into the enormity
of the heart, torn
from blind comfort
into the harsh glare
of time   and fate.

Hard to know
how to be true to one's own heart
without causing pain—
I stand between my two hearts
  passion and
  uncertain annihilation
knowing that
  the agent of pain
  is the death of pleasure

How to be true
  without causing sorrow
I search for it
and, finding I've failed,
it pierces me.

Yearning to hold you
and soothe you
and whisper sweet words to you
to ease the torment of the twisted heart.
the lover become daemon
distorting into fragments
of un-known origin.

Not knowing, now
how what is found, becomes lost
And what seemed good
  and almost holy
becomes the source
of such agony.

How to cease railing against destiny
  to reside
in the stillness
of the moment
between passion
and despair.

The song sang something
about acceptance—
an elusive air, calling me
toward suspension of desire,
revealing all things, caught
in an inheld breath

# *Siren's Call*

Pain cascaded down
and the light receded
to a distant, twisting memory
The siren's call, dirge now,
tolling the wreckage

And I, in my wonder still,
at the cost of loving
too deeply—
hoping, against all reason
you will find your way home

Fear, a shrill siren
echoing ages past
of un-known victims
slain by unseen hands

Waiting for the pain to settle,
the landscape shook too violently;
the snowflakes still cover
the edges, obscuring
my view to you

Not knowing who
you will be to me
as the last snowflake falls.
Guilt, like icicles
piercing fevered dreams

I can but hold you in my heart
and dream away your pain
not knowing if I've become
intrusion, or some second skin
welcomed or disdained

I will, against all reason,
toward the day
when the snowflakes settle
and the lava cools, enough
to sort through the wreckage

and recover, some trace
of that lost civilization
arising anew
like phoenix from the ashes
transformed

wiser now, enough perhaps,
to not enflame that mountain
and send its contents spilling—
molten lava, freezing slowly
into piercing muted screams

Disbelief staggers me
I stand frozen, looking back
Alive to the sweetness
of paradise lost
willing, against the fall

already come, hoping
to believe in resurrection;
Carrying dreams of memories
toward the uncertainty
of safekeeping.

# *Crashing to the Shore*

I come crashing
to the shore
treasure or refuse
I am not sure

Pummeled and spewn
by such tremendous forces
one can only yield
to their greater power

And in the yielding
find one's own
in the very act
of submission.

Years of pounding
against the sands
have smoothed even
my most jagged contours

I no longer wish
so fervently
to be other
than I am

More fascinated, now,
by the paths winnowed
by receding waters
leaving patterns in the sand.

Standing silent,
whipped by wind's embrace
caressed by tiny tentacles
curling wavelets at my feet

Drinking deeply
the inland waters
of sea stretching outward
toward infinity.

Such tiny creatures, we,
scurrying madly against despair
  embryonic tributes
to a force greater still

Yet standing firm and steadfast
in our willingness to yield
to the impenetrable
and find ourselves anew.

# *Judas*

I have become Judas
betraying with a kiss
what should have been left
sacred for all eternity

How is it
that such pure passion
of spirit becomes tainted
by the world's intrusion

Or does
the purity of spirit
become tainted
by the passions' rule

Perplexed by a world
in which love becomes condemned
I hang on the gallows
of your recoil

Cast out
into a role
presaged by the sadness
of the icy grip of fear

Cast in
to this odd role of betrayer
fingering the strange raiment
like a second skin

Leaving no room
but to rail
against the ravages
of time   and distance.

# *Leaving April*

The fever has broken
leaving in its wake
the illusion of coolness
of fevered dreams, passing into disbelief

Standing now,
on uneasy ground
like a colt
on tentative, awkward feet

Poised on the threshold
of a world
no longer ruled
by that strange passion

taken hold
with such intensity
there was no
letting go.

Truth becomes
an uneasy ally
in the face of
steep pitched dreams

as we toss
and turn within them
becoming tangled
in the sheets

of some new reality.
I gasp deeply
against the absence of air
and submerge myself within

that strange world
of chords playing
against my senses
in haunting melodies.

Knowing
at some level
that one does not survive long
in that rarefied air

and yet, to swim once again
in that strange ocean
buoyed aloft
by the salty spray

of tears not yet shed
carries me away
until the icy plunge
descending me

into some other's reality,
demanding my return
from that land
of waking dreams.

I am tossed on its shore
carelessly, flotsam now,
from dis-owned
un-remembered dreams

gasping for breath
from lungs become gills
in those moments
outside time

when fevered dreams
re-worked my interiors
into some strange hybrid
I barely recognized.

The siren's call
becomes my own voice
luring me out
toward such deep waters

I could but lose my way
hoping against all reason
for safe passage
to some unseen shore

where I might
dislodge these waters
from lungs stretched
beyond all recognition.

Discharged so violently
from the water's grip,
become an assault
upon the shore

transforming slowly
into the familiar warmth
of sand tracing patterns
in the ebbing tides.

Odd to stand
naked here once more,
yet I have learned
to love these furrows

and gullies shaped
by standing in the wind,
singing songs half-remembered
from the chords of fevered dreams

newly forged
in the coolness and infinite patience
of the hand that soothes
the fevered brow

I stand before my ocean
and cast forth my songs as hymns
No net now, no siren's call;  Only dreams
tempered, toward the sanctity of safe passage.

# *Time Travel*

I know that leap
as I watch her take it
gloriously, with trepidation,
tuned to the inward aching
toward unimaginable union

I swim vicariously in her sea
exquisitely tuned   to the play between
her vantage and my own,
willing back the withering,
time's journey into crone

Time travel on my daughter's wing
has taken varied forms
launched safe within
my wizened shell,
this crucible of years

She comes to me for knowing,
truth not yet revealed,
as she journeys
with such innocence
beyond my veil of tears

Soothing in the solace
of our gazes thus entwined
glows her beauty evanescent,
lends her dreams
a mirrored shine

I have known her as I know my self,
endlessly repeating,
in the vastness
of this cosmic joke
increasingly un-known.

# *New Age Alchemy*

She waits for something
to come from nothing
a tribute to
her new age alchemy

Shadowing the silence
In the moment
she becomes it—
human flesh fed on air

A wild thinness rages
in her body, ranging
toward the predatory
become prey   her own flesh,

whose cells she wills frozen
in this dream time
in the spaces   in between
living and dying

She has waited so long
the banquet has withered
on a table now festooned
by thin wisps of dry webs

No place set for her
at the table
there was no place
not already taken, by the queen

That regal presence
whose reign endured
all these years
even beyond her passing

No time left, not tainted
by that tyrant's rule
become order, in the disordering
of a child's dream—
new age alchemy   subdued.

Marilyn Charles

# *Uncertain Physics*

I step from icy floe to floe,
inwardly calculating
the motion of unseen forces
massing platelets from the earth's core

Staggered by the incalculable geometry
of the dance of planets
played to an unheard melody
beyond my fathoming

I listen, still,
for the soundless whispers
in an unknown key
intoning my history

Some vast and infinite scheme
eludes my view
ordained by chance patternings
of flesh in fluid

The word becomes flesh
finding its own voice
ostensibly, yet still enslaved
by the urgency of time

in the piper's tune.
I'd known these faults and mires,
dancing over them fluidly
in the face of my desires

Until the notes shattered
in the coldness of the air
and the stillness deafened me
and I could not hear

my own voice, calling me
back   into these distant dreams
traversing the galactic stairs
once patterned by the moon and air.

# *The Quest*

My son sets off upon his quest
forged in fluid and tempered by fire
At his throat, his mother's amulet
his father's sword upon his side.

What unknown call lures him toward
the strange rhythms of unknown rhymes
no longer fashioned by the father's tongue
nor fathomed in the mother's eye

Fate flings him forward over alien ground
driving relentlessly toward the distance
beckoned by the new moon rising
blood orange in the summer sky

Pledging fealty to some new master
dimly visioned in the sparkle of an outstretched hand
by eyes blinded as the moon's glare outshines
the erstwhile brilliance of sun's rays.

I watch his heart carry him, relentlessly
toward the vast ache of distance, beyond my view
in pledge of this new season, wrestled
from the grip of rocking horse and nursery rhyme

A tale told too often, this heart's quest
for a visioned horizon beyond my own,
valiantly unwilling to be less than a meteor
hurtling   across the night sky.

# *Fragments*

I pore over these fragments of images
trying to find the whole in the part
Catching part of me
loses the whole of me
in successive iterations
spanning centuries
of womankind
withered
by blatant un-knowing
of her essence.

I move within this tiny shell
to trace the journey from my beginnings
not knowing where it will end
save ultimately
in un-knowing
un-feeling
un-being.

But, for now,
there is this vacuum
in between
the non-being
which becomes everything
in the moment of communion
with the conception
of the shell.

# *Uncertain Physics ii*

i

My heart becomes a fulcrum
between love and despair
desperately trying
for some uneasy balance
bifurcating into two arcs
describing wide oscillations
into the madness
of separate lives
iterated in uneasy branchings
of irrational equations
outside the reaches
of rational mind
in the dream time.

ii

Perhaps this new science
will help explain
these wide oscillations
bifurcating my energies
into twin arcs
of urgent trajectories
projecting outward
beyond any will
or intention
leaving me suspended
on a fulcrum
between passion and desire
on either side
the labyrinthian twists
of urgent calls
to witness   blazoning
the morning light
and evening sky.

Marilyn Charles

# *Endlessly Repeating*

In a dream
of endless streets and
impossible passageways,
endlessly repeating,
I find you
  and lose you
and find you once again,
in recurring patterns
of almost seen glimpses
of diaphanous silk
whipping lazily
across empty windows
of translucent glass
dimly seen
  through the veil of dreams

In the dream time
you are here and gone
in the same instant.
I turn, and almost see
what remains
  always elusive,
never held in gaze

Sleep becomes the passage
through the mirror
into my alter-image—
my waking dreams
become real.

I keep searching,
  willing to find you
in those streets
  so strangely familiar
they taste of dimly recalled
  long forgotten memories
of sights not seen
  and paths not taken.

# *Wrinkles*

An unseen hand
pulls at the wrinkles
in the fabric of time
stretched unevenly,
upending the players
and sending them reeling
mercilessly
to their knees.

Please tell me
how beauty becomes distorted
into the cacophony
of splintered fragments
shifting crazily
until truth becomes
one more thread
in illusion's web.

# *Evanescence*

To catch the moment
and hold it
like an iridescent globe
spinning   on cautious fingertips
displaying its brilliance, for an instant,
then gone

I hold it, hovering,
until my inheld breath
releases, whispering,
toward the sun.

Dreams dance, reflected,
entering airily
that rare atmosphere
concocted by a child's
most earnest whim.

Such magic can only be marveled at
yet we chase it like children
delighting in the soapy kiss
of moistness
on cheek and lips

We run to meet the day
not yet turned solemn
by somber clouded eyelids
slanted stiffly
into blind arches
of archaic dead desire

The bubble bursts
into the infinity
of childhood tears

Eternity's despair shifts
as the light catches
glistening
some new iridescent image
reflecting sun beams
dry the tears.

# *Solitary Tear*

The solitary tear
descends its facets
down a face

slicing slender furrows
of dis-ease
planted permanently now

into silent accusing stares
that meet
in passion turned to stone

I have searched for you
on distant hillsides
but cannot find you, here

in this frozen landscape
of cold
and solitary isolation

Once-warm breath
turns to vapor,
in icy fragments.

Turn to me now
the one blind eye
made whole by adoration

Evasive, now elusive,
against these rhythmic,
aching contractions

of a birth
older than time
intruding into the fabric

sewn with care and wonder
rent now,
by tears of sorrow

and disbelief
heralded in the eyes
of fallen angels

Marilyn Charles

# *Tonal Vibrations*

Expectant, I await
the tonal vibration
heralding your presence.

I know the tone I seek
It envelopes me
in the mystery of reunion.

Waiting now, I reach
down, into the recesses
of my silence
beneath the clatter
of urgency
  or desire
toward the moment
when hope stills
  toward acceptance
like the babe's first cry
piercing the silence
of anticipation

Thrust, reluctantly,
from the realm
of infinite possibilities
  into the confines
of linear time
and corporeal reality

Trying to carry
the imminence
of infinite harmonies
  unheard now
in this realm
of heavy chords

Strummed
by fingers
made awkward
from lack of faith
I flee from
its ponderous weight,

Sensing the air
for signs
of lighter currents
to carry me
  into the chord
sustained once more.

Marilyn Charles

# *Smoke*

I am smoke
evanescent images
filtering into your imaginings

Dream me into view
that I might see
how I become you

Like a flame
coiling, conforming
to your contours

Sniffing the strange scent
of life consumed
by passion's fire

Burning itself into embers
of red heat
white ash

Lingering traces of warmth
in the coldness
of night air

Fluidly unchanging
like water creatures,
prototypes of later forms

Unseen by the naked eye
yet speaking
of an implicit order

Startling in its simplicity
organic and flowing,
unfolding in strange syncopation

Beyond conception
such magnificent simplicity
insidiously beguiling

Mirroring unknown secrets
of an implicate order
in unfettered mind.

# *A Moment's Dream*

In a moment's dream, unfettered
by dis-remembered fragments
of events un-seen,
you appeared un-known
yet strangely familiar
evoking urgent whispers
of unheard melodies
almost captured
on the breeze.

I dive deeper
hoping to find my bearings
on this ocean shelf
become haven
for whatever spectre
becomes the casing
shielding memory
from unimaginable secrets
divined in dreams

The layers become steps
each their own reality
like some strange marketplace
redolent cacophony
of smells, sounds, and images
so confounded
that each becomes hidden,
lost within the refuge
of the din

Arriving now,
safely secreted
in the wealth of sensations
jubilant mis-affirmation
of unfathomable loss
at what cannot be found
in the con-founds
of past and future
within and without.

Marilyn Charles

# *On Refusing to Be Dead*

I find myself mourning
something not dead
  only the urgency of it
so palpably present
girding my loins
in rapture's warm embrace

Perplexed, I finger lovingly
pieces of dreams
  of long-ago and far-away
mysteries of meeting
so wondrous, even now
they take my breath away

I run to meet them,
stopped by furied winds
  beseeching temperance
I lose my way
in storms of shoulds
and recantations

Some storms too blinding
to see; evoking my own
  night blindness
cursed paucity
of faith's fire
fleeting

Till the winds still
and shadows part
  to eyes  now accustomed
to the dim echoes
of falling stars
caught in outstretched hands

From within the bowels
of deepest mourning
  thrashing blindly
I find myself yearning
toward the light
like moth to flame.

# *Shot*

You listen
into my darkness
silently sensing
for some index
of wind's direction
to carry you fatefully
into the ease of unknowing
or fitful waking dreams

I sense you watching
with this third eye
evolving
over light years
of photoscopic instants
developing
on your inner palate,
shades of me

Our waking selves
move forward
uttering inanities
semblances of sanity
suffered graciously
dissembling
shamelessly
in syncopated rhyme

Till your truth
shot my darkness
like an arrow
still quivering
in the deer's chest
like some odd
ornamentation
in silent humiliation

As the rules changed
  dispensed in time
passing beyond
boundaries transgressed;
silent lapse beyond
the confines
of the old order
  that safe border

now ransacked
by careless thieves
and unruly victims
unheeding
the ending whistle
as the film flaps
its unwieldy ending
on the killing floor.

We lie in darkness
waiting for the light
of yesterday gone
in the wake
of tomorrows
hotwired
before their time
  stolen forever

endlessly mourned,
hiding from the light
of truth shot
piercing the darkness
in that unrelenting
instant, seen
endlessly repeating
in the echoes of a dream

of faith affirmed
in love's illusions
  never lost
and sacrifice redeemed
in unbroken promises
of life's passions
  with no cost
and unfragmented dreams.

# *The Banquet*

I came into the empty room
unbidden by the mass
to marvel at the riches there
close beyond my grasp

I stole into her chamber
slipped silent like a thief
alone and all unbidden
into her reverie

I came the uninvited guest
intruder in the lair
to suckle on the silver spoon
and taste the wines of care

I fed upon the refuse
of dis-remembered dreams
repenting for the outrage
intrusion on the queen

What child is this who wanders
into the taken house
in silent accusation
of what is not allowed

Do penance for defilement
do penance for deceit
to weave the warp of intrigue
into the weft of dreams

She pierced upon their vision
endured the silent screams
atoned her bleak intrusion
in garment rent and mean

Do penance for the outrage
do penance for deceit
of entering unbidden
into the realm of dreams

I came upon the banquet
unbidden by the guests
to chronicle my story
and disavow the rest

I left the wine untasted
until I found my own
and closed the door quite softly
upon my erstwhile home.

# *Your Eyes*

Eyes encased
in walnut folds
of grace, extended—
ripples of a stone   thrown
some half century past

Soft cheek
unearthed from layers
of rubble frosted over
by time, then razed
toward youth's recapture

How daunts the gaze
of inward held eye
in the shrill mirror
and siren's light
warning of perfidy

Now emblazoned
in muted tongues
telling tales of joy and sorrow
to ears newly deafened
by discontent

My finger travels
in wonder down
fissures formed
into rivulets
of tears become flesh

Encoded in cryptic rhyme
onto skin once smooth
untraveled by care
the promise of a child's palm
in her mother's hand

My eye caresses
the fine emanations
webbed across your face
like sun's rays streaming
in a western sky

Illuminating vast vistas
in subtle desert hues
enraptured by the imminence
of storm clouds   gathering
beyond the horizon

Their radiance paled only
by the gaze itself
transfixing me, in reverence
at the artless candor
of such ageless innocence

Lines of torture
easing now
as the brilliance
of your recognition
illuminates my own.

# *Dance Lessons*

I am trying to learn this dance
in the absence of explicit rules
marking the meaning of motions
the significance of steps
taken—untaken—

How to understand
this thrust, that parry
is it a tango?
or a minuet?

I close my eyes
to imagine the music;
allow its rhythm
to overtake me,
hoping to divine
the right movement
from whatever opus
we are conducting.

Even the pause is pregnant
with meaning, ripe
in its evocations
too myriad
to fathom
much less fashion
the corresponding chord
in the correct key

as though there might be
a correct key
rather than
this elusive melody
infinitely transposing itself
in elaborate harmonies.

I stop
and press my ear
to the silence
haunting me

Are they only reverberations
of my own whispers
pulsating?

like echoes of the ocean
culled from a shell
in a child's ear?

I wait.
Moments like daggers.
The sharp stiletto
of a dancer's heel
thundering out
the impossible staccato
  blood rushing   too hard
insistent time   beating
into fevered temples
of desire

Cast adrift now,
as though disowned—
particles of unused dreams
floating lightly
like silk
on a breeze
in this kaleidoscope
of unknown melody

A duet
played
by one hand
in anticipation
of the next

I am trying to recapture
a melody
once heard,
long forgotten.

I whisper into the breeze
hoping to catch its echoes—
with no assurance
that the breeze blows true
from one shore to another—
or what it would say
save silence.

# *Traces*

I study the patterns
of an ebbing wave,
leaving whorls
like fingerprints tracing
sand-encrusted mysteries.

I poke at them
with my imaginings
hoping to discern
some prevailing order
before the next wave hits

Leaving new configurations
for my tried imagination
endlessly searching
   an erstwhile fortuneteller
reading tea leaves in a dish.

Like a child prods a turtle
seeking signs of reassurance
of the omnipresent life
retracted in the recess
of the smooth protective shell

Hidden from probing fingers—
my curious delight
at the wonder of discovery
lurks   this strange creature,
hidden, barely out of sight.

Crouching now,
like a child, caught
by the imminent revelation
too remote to fathom
too rough to comprehend

The confusion of disorder
becomes the new order
unfathomable at first
until the eyes accustom
to the new wave's leavings.

Continual repatternings
tax and trouble me
as I strain to discern
the path of history
from relics in the sand

Until, spent, I lean back
toward the sun's light, reflected
in hot auras on my lids
to bask   in the tireless wisdom
of the wind.

# *In Your Dreams*

In your dreams, I would
bring you fields of wildflowers
and cool mountain streams

and lay sweet garlands
of soft grass
to pillow your cheek

and soothe the lines of care
with enchanted whispers
calling you home to your self.

Into the crazed chaos
of clattering dis-order
come interspersions of silence

sweet sounds to sing you
back into your own key
when all without is disharmony.

My poor magic fails me
in the face of such cacophony
careening into your solitude

Leaving my poor hands empty
of any, save faery dust,
to trail across the moon

and bring sweet dreams
into your inner pool
rich reservoir of the soul singing.

Marilyn Charles

# *Between the Joy and Sorrow*

There is this layer
I've been searching for
between the joy and the sorrow
where neither is quite out of reach

I think you've found it
But then, it's easy to believe
in the illusions
we paste on our horizons
fluffed across the heavens
like a child's collage, with cotton
and sticky fingerprints
to betoken love's labor spent

I am left to watch
at a distance
and wonder who I see
and whether you will let me

Fear so constant
it feels like a friend
reminders of who we may be
within the bounds of acceptability

As though we did not see
those rough edges
in sharp relief
in the open doorway—
only as unloved
as we believe them to be

I would love those best
though I fear
you finding them in me
even knowing
they must be
most dear
to any lover's eye—

Fear of faith—to put it to the test
leaves the door closing
against us
  locked
within ourselves.

# *Fog*

So hard to find a poem in all this greyness
though I keep waiting for one to appear
as though, if I were just silent enough,
I could come upon it sleeping
and catch it unaware

Even the seeking becomes elusive
as the grey enfolds me in its mist
driving toward some vast mystery
arising in the denseness
of darkening air's elusive kiss

My back turns, in effigy of feigned indifference
drawn long since on an upturned breath
sighed into the darkness,
dreaming vague images
sodden in the unfallen rain

Who was she, might have been,
had she not become me so unwittingly
I hadn't even known of whom I dreamed
till the dreamer turned
and it was me.

Unknowing, she lingered, crooning lullabies
and dark dirges in an unknown tongue
awaiting the memory
of inchoate lies
awakening, to set her free

So hard to find a poem in all this greyness
I travel lightly—on cat's feet
longing for vision yet wrapped in oblivion
fearing the awakening
of long abandoned memories

Marilyn Charles

# *Behind the Gate*

Intently, you search for me
behind this visage
frozen
in the silence
of despair

You probe
for mode of entry
into that
at times forbidden territory
to which you've passed so often
yet never held the key

The sentry being given to caprice
in his movements—
it is never quite clear
where he will travel
  always some distance
from wherever last seen

In the intervals between rounds
you seek the opening
to the space so familiar,
though whereabouts unknown,
always a relief,
though surprised,
to find yourself at home

Beyond my arms' embrace
you seek the inner movement
of wings beating
reciprocal patternings
onto your own

To find me at the threshold
of a dance
not yet created
nor even imagined
in latter day dreams.

# *That Love Endures*

Even in the fullness of my sorrow
I cannot sanction regret
for one impetuous moment
driving as it did
toward destiny

In the throes of loss, I wonder
and finger longingly
toward a tendril of your hair
fallen unnoticed
across your cheek

Your oblivion as dear
as the acuity of your gaze
resting on some unfathomable truth
made less obscure in the light
of life-years of restless soul seeking

I think of you now, slumped in your chair
weighted by the impossibility
of being true to twin brides of warring lands
each calling to you
in their own tongue

Rocking you relentlessly
in their keening rhyme: asynchronic disharmony
with no mercy for the figure battered
in the bifurcation of elements
earth and fire, sea and air

Do you visit me, betimes, in waking dreams
unfettered by the harsh rays of search lights
now trained upon your visage
eating out your secrets   from syringes
implanted in the soft flesh
hidden under tidy fingernails

Even in the racking pain of silent sorrow
echoing across the void
careening wildly across sheer surfaces
newly forged
in fear and loathing—

Even in the ache of emptiness
as lungs strain for the rhythm of rarefied air—
I wander in the shadows
as eyes accustom to the tonal illumination
of richly patterned darkness

And wonder at the icy treasures
growing in this hollow cavern become prison wall
with no substance, only the subtle power
of the word barring entry
to a land once mine

Oddly,
even in the aching jaws of eternity's chasm
there is faith's promise
that love endures
beyond all boundaries
  and artifice
  and vanities
  and sorrows

that love endures.

# *God's Finest Moment*

This must have been
God's finest moment—
the miraculous creation
of union
communion   of souls
embodied
into charged particles
at rest

The feel of flesh on flesh
the heat of your body
and the energy between us
dancing
in intricate whorls
like arabesques patterned
onto the icy surface
of deep water
filling the moment
so completely

I am in awe
at the vast complexity
that could have conjured
this particular configuration
of pain and passion
  ecstasy and despair
  absence and presence
that becomes the union
between man and woman.

# *Headlights*

My search for poems draws me now
so deep inside, the silence is barely audible
Within these dark spaces there is no poem—
only the sadness of the resting place
left behind   when my words shrieked
into the glaring light of sirens flashing
and blind drivers   smashing   horns blaring
their unified tribute to urgent despair.

The process became stillborn—or forcibly aborted—
as the assembly workers left their posts
to wonder at the cacophony created
by archaic symbols scrawled
against a printed page emitting
musky scents of love's labors washed
across the tendrils of petals waiting
for the sweet taste of morning's dew.

And now, the doe, startled by the havoc
wreaked in the face of her existence
  out of time, out of place,  stunned
beyond motion into the ongoing stall
of intolerance for displaced miracles
unearthed in odd places,   then un-found
suddenly, in the headlights flashing
sirens screaming and tempers raging.

Silenced, the crumpled paper falls
unnoticed by any, save the doe,
too saddened  to suffer  her stillborn child
in the face of such madness,   recedes
into the far forest of quiet thoughts
and magical incantations
of earth infused   by the gift of rain
absorbing into ripened leaves fallen.

# *A Poem for You*

I would like to find a poem for you
enchanting words, to flow
like water into wine
to wet the lips imagined
opened, parched for mine

I dream vast images into you
Whorls of swirling sensations
unique and mysterious
as fingerprints, etched
across a dark sky   in iridescent colors

I search my inner landscapes for the poem
'twould ease the lines of care
etched across your face
in wracking rhythms   I trace
the furrows of my despair

lightened, by each rising sun
bringing me closer to your voice
echoing anew into the emptiness
of time suspended
in this amazing void

Walls   so vast,
the edges of them seep
their tired memories
of unshed tears
coursing like sweat
into the darkness.

I yearn for the poem
to hold you, even in this vast desert
of time unspent
and wine untasted
the eucharist lost

through the gaping cracks
of uncertain steps
The enormity of grief
The absurdity of blindness
The tragedy of lost moments.

I would like to sing a song for you
to whisper as you sleep
  that time is not eternal
  that life is not a dream
rolling onward toward forever

in a lush unbroken stream,
but seeps slowly, relentlessly
and trickles from our grasp
crashing, like cool water
savored,  or left, at last   untasted.

# *Memory Traces*

Memory traces, after your call,
linger disconcertingly;
what was said, and unsaid;
all the myriad nuances of voice
left unanswered, save in silence;
my unaspirated monologue
circling relentlessly
with no medium left for exchange.

The treachery of too little time
leaves no luxury for small intimacies:
the patterned interweavings
of your life, with mine
all flattened and left for dead
The urgency of momentous matters
of no real moment, in this moment
when time has ceased, leaving us immobile
in separate galaxies.

I wish to have received your words
and lingered to savor your gifts,
but they only screamed to me
of a life going on without me.
And thrust aside, impatiently,
to see what is left of mine,
losing you in my carelessness,
as you reply, in kind,

leaving no air in the dark cavern
for the songbird lying too tired
to call, even were there ears to hear
silent tears wracking breasts
unmoved by years of waiting
to speak into the silence
and be heard, unheard;
swallows bitter
spewing coal dust and dark ashes.

Wouldst to have flown upward,
before the descent became too dizzying
lost in the labyrinth of tears waiting,
the shrill braying of lost souls seeking companions.

So hard to know—till too late enters,
shaking the rain from its cloak,
  knowing the deluge has just begun
with no sign of passing; each pause another stake
in the heart of a dying vampire.

# *Learning to Live Without You ii*

Learning to live without you
has been
like decompressing
oxygen
out of lungs
mutating
toward survival
in unfamiliar air.

Traveling a landscape,
foreign
yet familiar
configured
by old dreams
in new images
breathtaking
in their power.

In the silence
between breaths
cascade
fallen images
  ill-begotten dreams
untasted
frozen now
in cold pageantry.

The wistfulness of wanting
  cruel luxury now
as planets
sheer past
vying
for some new order
in a universe gone mad
with waiting

for the taste of air
not yet caught
by the compaction
of a throat
closed
by absent longing
toward a past   lost
to the greedy rasping
of dry lungs.

# *To Leave This Past Behind*

To leave this past behind
I would swim silently,
in hard, even strokes
toward some horizon,
remote and dimly imaged
  shrouded in the mists
of unshed tears,
falling relentlessly,
in splintered fragments
refracting in the sun's glare
to gently mingle with salty spray
becoming memories.

Legs taut in their patterned rhyme,
urgently,  leaving behind
all trace of lost labours
trampled under blind feet
beyond any hope of recognition
  like leaves becoming earth
in forest's paths;
the painful taint of childhood
carried on an east wind
washing over me, like dreams,
almost tasted, like an oasis,
ever distant;  ever near.

I swim toward that horizon
with strokes measured
in grim determination
as though to prove its existence
or nonexistence;  splitting firmly
  harsh waters of being,
closing relentlessly
even as I pass
through swells of certainty,
in the sun's assurance
and the darkening eddies
  the daughter's despair.

Stroking firmly   through
waters icy in the sheer depth
of bottomless space, looming,
calling from the dark void
of the harshness of being,

firmament lying hidden
behind illusion, like a mountain
lost to sight
beyond the vastness
of a child's hand held tightly,
warding off the looming mass
towering against a grey sky

toppling, relentlessly,
as the winds shift
and the seas mount
and I stroke outward
toward the breakers   and beyond
into the calm of mystery,
density of deep waters,
calling, in rhythmic, lapping rhyme
toward some safe horizon
dimly imaged as shifting cards
shuffle in an unwieldy deck
held in an unsure hand.

I swim, solitary now,
save a lone gull's call,
bones unchilled by icy fathoms;
skin unwarmed
by sun's deep rays
in an ocean once full of mystery
and sweet anticipation
barred now, by the dulling of years
and the hardening of hope
into the weighted dullness
of cold facts, dotting the landscape,
leaving little room
for the sweet taste of dreams.

# *Altars of Oblivion*

I turn away
to find my self
waiting
once again
in the small room
at the top of the stairs
icons in attendance
  placed perfectly
building altars of oblivion
  in alcoves of despair
awaiting the lone acolyte
who breathes new life
into archaic rituals

creating from the wreckage
the mystery of meaning
and wonder
at the severance
of self from other
become
the ostensible price
  of admission
to this strange shrine
  anointed with odd relics
strewn in immaculate dis-order
toward a new god
of archaic imaginings.

I pray at this altar,
wistfully; toward some remote,
elusive harmony
emptying my self
of my self
toward re-union
  with some immaculate stranger
born
  of cast-off imaginings
in this cell
in which I sever
my being from yours
toward ultimate salvation.

# *Finding a Fantasy*

I wonder who it is
this person you find in me

I turn
as though to catch
that visage
over my shoulder
before she turns
to stare over her own
in a movement
infinitely repeating

I thought you had found me—
not knowing it was never me
only some illusion of your self
you had been seeking

Was that my truth too?
Did I stop short of you
content to find my own image
hidden within your outer confines

From this distance,
the little disappointments
speak of vast chasms
that felt almost like meeting

If only I'd known the right words—
not knowing there were no right words
that could have ricocheted between us
without losing meaning in each shadow

Sometimes, finding a fantasy
is only that—and nothing more
and dissipates in the distance
like waking from a dream.

Marilyn Charles

# *Doors Closing*

You welcome me in
then close, door after door,
in endless succession,
doors slamming
as they open,
beguiling in their mysteries
wafting scents of unglimpsed gardens
shimmering in the afterglow
almost seen.

Beneath the clatter, I hear
gulls calling on ocean breezes
careening toward the sun
in breathless flight
behind doors shutting endlessly,
like dominoes falling,
until time is suspended
in the eerie light between
yesterday and tomorrow.

In between times
I wander, through
oddly darkened skies and light
reflected from yesterday's passing
leaving dreams of fantasies
half-remembered in the dusk
of spirit, roaming
between desire and release
from her open cage.

# *Fallen Leaves*

Fallen leaves
clutter the darkness.

Last fruits of the season
dry forgotten on the vine.

Hands burrow into deep pockets
seeking shelter from the winds'
bitter turn

Shoulders hunched against the weight
of too many seasons passing
to clearly remember any

Only lingering fragments
like leaves falling
or memories of scents upon a breeze

Sloughing relentlessly
through the sad debris
of spring's promise

and summer's finest hour

Forgotten refuse now,
a crush of fallen leaves.

# *Fallen Leaves ii*

Fallen leaves rustle
on empty streets (unnoticed)
like yesterday's news

Fasten your windows
tight—against the night air come
seeping through the cracks

Draw close your curtains
against the longings of
the creatures of the night

Hold fast embattled
dreams against the bitter wind
rapping at the panes

Secure your memories
against receding footsteps
haunting at your door.

# *Fireworks*

The meeting
exploded
into fireworks
of such rare beauty,
senses reeled
leaving little room
for any
called common

Thrust
into a new dimension
of such exquisite
pleasure
  pain
with little way
of gauging safety
by inner compass

made useless
by the extraordinary
magnetism
of two minds
synchronized
into strange harmony
of darkness—and light
thrust ever deeper

A mythic forest
of wondrous limbs
and musky scents
overgrowing all senses
in one wondrous symphony, poised,
a lone true note in still air
vibrating its harmonies
into infinity

The meeting was magic
painted in lush undertones
untasted, too saturated
to even register
except in retrospect
then savored slowly
in mirror pools of reminiscence
fingered lovingly

like iridescent eddies
in a still stream.

Sheathed in unheard harmonies
once promised;   in a spring breeze
haunting all melodies—
delights anticipated
recede untasted—
summer's brief bounty
withers on a vine
untended

As we lost our way together—
the path became too solitary
sounding notes into a cold distance
echoing painfully,  the chilling,
now reverberating absence
despair of defiance
aching towards
renunciation

I strike the lone chord,
reminder of the still surround
echoing into oblivion
empowered by the stillness
gathering into me
its solitary sustenance
distilling emptiness
into virtue

The inheld breath
becomes possibility
  suspended moment;
the alchemist's dream
  awaiting redemption
  condensation of desire
profusion of particles, scattered
in a passing breeze.

# *A Poem for You ii*

You ask for a poem
and stand, hopefully,
wistfully, at the doorway
separating
your world from mine.

You bid me weave   an opening
of time and space   suspended
that you might pass through
seamlessly, effortlessly
to sit in the crook of my imagination
  for a moment
and rest there forever

becalmed from whatever cares
left traces in the fine furrows
radiating from the corners
of eyes too numinous
to fathom.

I brush soft whispers of fingertips
to infuse these emanations,
yet not disturb the pathways
but only rest there, briefly,
in the depth of your gaze.

You ask for my leave
to sit inside my dreams
—as I coil into your own—
stroking the sybil's locks
as she weaves
filaments of fantasies
into your imaginings

in sweet lullabies sung
to the dirge
of dark waters, closing
relentlessly, just beyond reach
as your imminence recedes
in each instant towards
the vastness in between.

But lie here, now, in this moment
As I stroke your hair
and sing sweet certainties
from a tear drenched throat
in notes falling like unmade promises
cascading like fountains
streaming songs of forever

In tales of lives unlived
save for moments outside time
when we burrow more deeply
into each other's soul
and plant our seeds
and see what manner
of mystery might grow

Close your eyes and dream with me
your moments into mine
as I weave them into tapestries
for shelter, in these arms
that long to hold you,
lying safe in your imaginings
as you abide in mine.

# *A Melody*

I would weave for you a melody
harp strings strum to thrill the air,
fountains of moonbeams,
cascading crystals, running icy cold
in deep basins of desire

No words in this rarified air
only vain attempts to capture
the trilling of atoms playing
to the evocation of a mutual presence
suspended in time

Strummed on a lyre
of such sweetness
tuned to the inner keening
of voices so deep
I am lost in listening

As the warmth infuses silent limbs
aching for a touch
to last a moment's fullness
echoing into silence
then re-struck

And carried—this lone note
tolling for the lost ship   sailing
farther from home
tolling for the sorrow   of sailing
farther   from home.

Marilyn Charles

## *Where I Have Been*

You ask where I have been
But, having passed through that gate
where words might be spoken
I have none
only empty wisps of air
pockets of emptiness
mouthed into the silence
like inverted smoke rings
captured
in a cloud of darkness

Your eyes wonder
at the absence of mine
quite painfully—
  should I catch them unaware—
of how caught I would become
by their shadow
  seeping
into the coldness gathering

You recede
in your uncertainty
having failed to find
whatever illusion
had been lost
as I ricocheted wildly
off truths
you could not fathom
  careening wildly
  into oblivion

Sweet vacuum
becoming distended
into eternities
of timeless space and
shapeless,
unendurable
instants
of endless time
tolling, receding
like the wake of a tide
not yet turned
but only gathering,
devouring, churning

the endless debris
of a lifetime
into infinite particles
of ocean
biting salt tears
on my tongue,
with no sting of familiarity
to remind me
of the eyes emptied
by my own blind stare
held, in desperation
like a cross to a vampire
  unseen
in the moment of light
  glancing
Shrill fingers shrieking loudly
in the silent stare.

No words
to save you
from the empty queues
gathering
inside the silence
No soft whispers
to soothe the furrows
once etched lightly,
now with a hard chisel
drawn unrelenting
our despair.

No salvation here,
no sweet lies
to hasten sleep
only the harsh contours
of nightmares
galloping relentlessly
toward an uneasy dawn.

# *From My Mother's Closet*

Decompressing in this odd reliquary;
ancient altar to an understanding
ever out of reach, held by the authority
of frozen smiles, playing round
the edges of death's disavowal

Poring through soft fabrics hanging,
mind's eye seeking, peeking
into boxes closed against fingers, prying;
Small safe-cracker, tuning to memories, probing,
playing colored strands like rosaries

Last rites of refuse, corrupting
thick white piles of carpet, concealing
a child burrowing, hiding, seeking
signs of solace behind closed eyes
penetrating her mirrored shrine

My heart pulls through strings like fingers,
whispering prayers like dreams, returning,
called by my own keening, fingers kneading
ridge points of meanings, eroding into vestiges
of memories, reworked from primordial clay

Sitting alone, supplicant once again
at the feet of clothing grown too big
for your body; Fingering fabrics
like discarded prayer wheels, singing songs of lament
through fingers tuned to the inner keening of despair

No one left to bar the door, I sit, circling backward
to the point of entry, playing out my destiny;
The Interloper, standing in the wings, unwanted;
gazing silently onto scenes already cast;
stigmata of the outcast spreading like a flush

Inhabiting forbidden spaces; plundering the refuse
of your dreams, once enlivened by desire,
dismissed, disowned, disremembered:
building sandcastles, commemorating myths
once dreamed in sweet whispers and soft lullabies

Too many memories for one life, yet we capture them,
like prisoners, till we too are chained by the ghostly voices,
haunted by mysteries too shocking to be taken whole;
Peering sideways, clutching the edges and believing
in the firmness anchoring frightened fingertips

Knowing you invented me to wash away the tears
of defeat; deceit; Holding me hostage to your retreat,
marking me: the "I" your defiant cry in the darkness
as you pierced my eyes: In fear? In hatred?
the I sitting huddled in your sanctum

Immolated, I hung for many years, bleeding
out my emptiness onto that cold white frost
covering the stain spreading just below,
as destiny entered, like partners exchanged
in some odd dance of the dead

Until you were too frail to keep me at bay
and allowed me entry, in your passing
to the empty space created by the absence of
your desire; your hatred; your love;
lost in the growing twilight

I sit, child again, in your full empty closet
trying you on, now that your presence
no longer bars me entry, but in your absence
I find you, whispering memories
transposed across the generations

Returning in successive seasons, seeking
treasure undiscovered in repeated gleanings
till the chaff sits sadly; unloved relics
once enlivened, now poignant, emptied
in her absence, with no power, as she fades.

Marilyn Charles

# *All Hallows*

I have been mourning your passing
for some time now
in strange archaic dances
against the dying flames
of a ritual bonfire
leaping across the night sky
throwing shadows across the heavens
obscuring even the most familiar
of constellations.

Inscrutable images
charted upon a palette of diamond colored hues
cut sharply from the tears of angels
drying in despair
thrown across a canvas too vast to fathom
or even follow
the intricate, impenetrable order
of lives written in the light years of dying stars.

Under those heavens,
the unbegotten child awaits the unknown order
to infuse ashen limbs
towards a forgotten movement
passed along the generations in hushed whispers
of aging mothers
bequeathing dying secrets to unknown daughters
through the language of the stars

Unvoiced promise whispered on the air
of ripening buds and drowsy bees and
rustling leaves falling towards a new order.
In the pungency of leaping flames and dying embers
lie vestiges of a memory lost too soon
to ever recall, but only surge forward
towards its promise, whispered, unknown,
through that dying vessel.

I have been restless, seeking
across inner constellations
too vast to fathom, for vestiges
of a fallen star, ricocheted too soon
—out of sight, out of mind—
to ever quite grasp or hold
some worried remnant
of that mirrored shine.

I have been mourning my passing
for some time now
in strange archaic dances
against the dying flames
of a ritual bonfire
leaping against the night sky
throwing shadows across the heavens
obscuring even the most familiar
of constellations.

# *Acknowledgments*

This book owes its origins to a life that left me thinking through sensations and images onto the page. I am forever grateful to Judith Harris and Walter Kravitz for their faith in me as a poet and artist. Their belief in me has helped me believe in myself. Judith has been an extraordinary source of support in encouraging me and helping me find a home for this work.

I want to thank all those at Mission Point Press who have helped to bring this volume to life. Their patience, persistence, and expertise have been much appreciated.

Finally, I am grateful to the family and friends who make life worth living. We do best when we are all in it together.

# About the Author

Marilyn Charles is a psychologist and psychoanalyst at the Austen Riggs Center, co-chair of the Association for the Psychoanalysis of Culture and Society (APCS), and Scholar of the British Psychoanalytic Council. Affiliations include the Chicago Center for Psychoanalysis, Universidad de Monterrey, Harvard Medical School, and the Association for Psychosocial Studies.

Marilyn lived in Spain, Switzerland, and the Netherlands during her early adolescence, affording a growth-enhancing disruption to her Midwestern childhood. Exposure to diversities of culture and the musicality of languages informed her love of art, language and literature, and her psychoanalytic interest in the aesthetic underbelly of life as lived. Her artwork was featured at the George Mason University Gallery and in her book chapter, "Remembering, Repeating, and Working Through Collage: Piecing Together the Fragments of Traumatic Memory," in DellaPiettra's *Perspectives in Creativity*.

During her young adulthood, Marilyn lived on the Navajo Nation. Exploring those history-rich terrains of subtle colours and nuance helped her heal from the too-much of urban existence, and informed her research interests, which include creativity, the intergenerational transmission of trauma, and the impact of devaluation on women and other marginalized groups.

She is committed to mentoring future generations of psychoanalytic scholars, clinicians, and researchers, and has consulted with many groups including Gunawirra, in New South Wales, and has presented her work nationally and internationally.

Currently, Marilyn resides in the Berkshires with her life partner and enjoys visits to her home and gardens by her son, daughter, son-in-law, grandchildren, and cherished family and friends.

www.ingramcontent.com/pod-product-compliance
Lightning Source LLC
Chambersburg PA
CBHW021325060726
47591CB00006B/1880

* 9 7 8 1 9 6 8 7 6 1 8 0 6 *